I am looking at the interface between the space and the object.
———— Chika OHGI

Authors: Keiko Kawashima, Laurel Reuter, Chika Ohgi
Series Editor: Matthew Koumis
Project Manager: Keiko Kawashima
Translator: Kaeko Nakagawa (and Stefana McClure p.38)
Graphic Designer: You. Kobayashi
Illustrations by Chika Ohgi
Reprographics by Fotoriproduzioni Grafiche, Verona, Italy
Printed in Italy by Grafiche AZ

Published by
Telos Art Publishing
PO Box 125, Winchester
SO23 7UJ
England
telephone: +44(0)1962 864546
facsimile: +44(0)1962 864727
e-mail: editorial@telos.net
U R L : www.arttextiles.com

© **Telos Art Publishing 2001**

ISBN 1-9020-152-58

A CIP catalogue record for this book is available from The British Library

Artist's acknowledgements
This book is dedicated to my son Atsushi Ohgi.
Special thanks to Koichi Kawashima.

Publisher's acknowledgements
With many thanks to all those who have helped in the production of this book, including Adriana Mosqueira, Ian Chalmers, Sue Leahy, Katherine James, Alessandra, Simone and Ermanno.

front cover illustration: *fragment of paper*
kozo, ganpi, pulp, cotton thread, needle
photo by You. Kobayashi

back cover: *thin ice*
ganpi, cotton thread
photo by You. Kobayashi

Portfolio Collection
Chika OHGI

TELOS

Foreword

Laurel Reuter

In 1993 I curated the exhibition Light and Shadow: Japanese Artists in Space. Chika Ohgi was one of a dozen artists who came to North Dakota to install her work. Over the years I had noted that artists in Japan approach installation differently than those in Europe and the United States. Japanese artists don't just install their work in three-dimensional space, instead they create the work with space itself as an equal presence. In Ohgi's art, paper and space are counterparts, one dependent upon the other for definition. In her world elements such as trees and humans, light and shadow, or air and water, co-exist, none dominating the others. Likewise, the seen and the felt are equals – nothingness has its own presence. This sense of integration and harmony informs everything she creates. As in music, the pauses, or spaces between, are as important as the notes or sounds.

There is an elegance, a lightness of being, and a sense of pure abstraction in her paperworks that also resembles music. In music the blocks of sound are so insubstantial that the listener counts on repetition to grasp the composer's intent. Similarly, each unit of paper in one of Ohgi's works is so ethereal that only when installed in mass is the viewer able to ascertain the whole.

The German philosopher Schopenhauer once mused that music is entirely independent of the phenomenal world, ignores it altogether. The American composer Roger Sessions went on to say that music communicates in a marvelously vivid and exact way the dynamics and the abstract qualities of emotion, but any specific emotional content must be supplied from without by the listener. Within the visual arts Ohgi's installations come closest to this total sense of existence within abstraction, emotion without emotional content. Art this highly evolved, this sophisticated, becomes a balm to the human spirit. This is what makes one return to the work of Chika Ohgi over and over again, what makes the viewer want to follow her artistic career, to know what she will do next.

Laurel Reuter
Director
North Dakota Museum of Art, USA

1 | floating grass
at North Dakata Museum
of Art, USA
1994

ローレル・ロイター

1993年、私は企画展「光と影ー空間における日本の作家」を行った。扇千花はそのときノース・ダコタを訪れた十二人の作家のうちの一人である。もう何年も前から、私は日本人作家のインスタレーションに対するアプローチが他のヨーロッパやアメリカの作家のそれと異なることに注目していた。日本の作家はただ作品を三次元の空間に設置するのみに留まらず、彼等は作品と空間を等しい存在として扱う。そして空間と共に作品を創り上げるのだ。扇の作品では、紙によるオブジェと空間が相互関係にある。オブジェの存在が展示空間の存在感を、また展示空間の在り方がオブジェの存在感をそれぞれ強めている。扇の世界では、自然と人間、光と影、空気と水などの要素が互いにその存在を認め合う。だから決して一方が他方を圧倒してその存在感を危うくすることは無い。これと同様に扇にとって、実際に展示空間で目の当たりにする光景と、それを見て何を感じるかは等しい関係に在る。それはまるで、何も無い空間が空っぽであるにもかかわらず、「無」としての存在意義を持ち始めるかのようでもある。見た目には何も展示されていなかったとしても観客はやはりそこで何かを感じるのである。オブジェそのものと展示空間の融合そして調和が常にある。例えば音楽においても曲の随所に停止の部分、いわゆる間があり、これらも曲の一部として無くてはならない存在である。

扇の紙によるオブジェに一貫して見られる優雅さや軽やかさ、そして純粋に抽象的な在り方は音楽にも通じる所がある。音楽において個々の音は余り多くを語らない。

聴く者がそれらの音を拾う上で繰り返す部分を捉え、そこでようやく作曲者の意図が見えてくる。これと同じ様に扇の作るオブジェ一つ一つは非常に抽象的である。だからこそ、それらが大きな集団となって空間に設置された時にのみ、観る者はその作品としての存在感を確かめることができるのだ。

ドイツの思想家、ショーペンハウエルは音楽が知覚できる世界と全く切り離されているとしてそれらの存在を無視したのだった。それに対してアメリカの作曲家、ロジャー・セッションズは、音楽は聴く者に大変生き生きと、明確な形で伝わるということ、そしてそのパワーと情緒豊かさを唱えたうえで、より細かく具体的な表現は、聴く者によってそれぞれ生み出されるべきであるとした。視覚芸術の分野において、扇のインスタレーションは、その抽象的でありながらも最終的な展示によって、その全貌を明らかにするという点で音楽に近いと言えるかもしれない。細やかで情緒溢れるにも拘わらず、その情緒の中身に対してのあからさまな提示はない。こうして著しく進化し、且つ洗練された扇千花の芸術は我々人間の精神を癒すアロマセラピーと言えるかも知れない。これが観る者を魅了してやまない理由の一つであり、そしてまた我々が次回作に期待を寄せる所以であろう。

ノース・ダコタ美術館（アメリカ）館長
ローレル・ロイター

5

Contents

Obscure Space

Keiko Kawashima

The Japanese word *aimai* can be translated as *obscure*. Admittedly this word can have pejorative connotations - certainly in Japanese one would hardly use the word in a positive sense. And yet I would venture to affirm that the art of Chika Ohgi is a study in obscurity, in ambiguity.

As a student, Chika Ohgi specialised in silk-screen printing. At that time, her work was always printed onto cloth. Gradually she became more interested in the cloth itself, and in particular in its edges, than in the techniques of printing onto the cloth. In cutting cloth she was always acutely conscious of its edge, of its border. Although this border could well be straight, it was nevertheless quite different from a line drawn by a sharp pencil for example. Ohgi explored various different impressions in those edges of cloth, and experimented with the use of bandages and narrow strips of cloth for her installations. However she felt restricted by the limited range of shape and size of cloth commercially available.

Ohgi's attention therefore soon wandered away from cloth and was drawn instead to paper, and in particular to Japanese paper. Made from plants with long fibres, Japanese paper has a particularly intriguing texture. This allows the artist to control the shape and size of paper best suited to her concept. In due course, she started making her own paper.

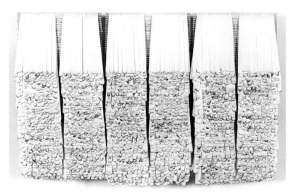

2 | paper field
  | 1986

First of all, though, she made *paper field*,[(Cat. 2)] an installation with bought paper whose edges she burnt. This work was nominated for the first international Textile Competition, Kyoto, in 1987. In this piece, she presented a contrast between the edge of the burnt paper and the original paper. With the exception of *paper field*, Ohgi's

彼女の求めている曖昧な空間

川嶋 啓子

日本語で「曖昧」という言葉は、英語では「Obscure」と言う言葉が与えられるのだろうか？またそれは、良い意味で取られるだろうか？もちろん日本語でもあまりいい意味で使う事は少ないけれども、あえて扇千花の作品は、あいまいさを求めている作品といいたい。何故あいまいなのかは後で述べることにして、先に彼女の作品の経過を見て行こうと思う。

彼女が最初に教育を受けた大学では、主にシルクスクリーンプリントの技術を学び、作品を制作してきた。そのプリントは、必ず布に施されていた。布にプリントをしているときに、彼女はプリントする技術よりも布に興味があった。そしてまた布の端（エッジ）に興味を持った。ある大きさに裁断された布は、まっすぐに裁断はされているけれども、糸のほつれが見え、よく見ると決してペンで書いたような一直線の線ではなく、それぞれが表情をもっていることに気がつく。また同時に、その布を空間にどう展示するかということにも、すでに興味をもっていた。その後、市販されている既製の布の端を意識した、空間構成の作品が続く。時には、包帯や短い巾の布を使っての空間構成があった。しかし、布には大きさや形の制限があることと、布の端の興味が紙、それも日本の和紙の紙の端に移って行く。まず、自分で紙を漉けば、自分がほしいと思っている大きさと形を手に入れることが出来るし、その大きさで彼女自身が空間の構成を決定出来る。日本の和紙は繊維質の長い植物を利用して出来ているので、手で1枚1枚漉かれた紙の端は、その時その時によって、すべてが全く違う表情を持っている事の興味であった。彼女は自然と自分で紙を漉く事を始める。自分で紙を漉く前には、市販されている紙のエッジを燃やし、それを並べて燃やされた端を強調する作品を発表し、この作品は1987年に開催された第1回国際テキスタイルコンペティション（図版2）に入選している。この時の作品は、燃やされた部分が黒く、ナチュラルカラーの紙との境界を

はっきりと醸し出している。しかしその後の作品は、ほとんど自分で漉いた紙を使っている。紙を漉くとその端は、柔らかな繊維が見え隠れしている。それを空中に吊ったり並べたりすると、その空間と紙の境界が曖昧になる。

扇千花は、その紙の決してナイフでカットされたようなシャープな端ではなく、漉かれた紙の柔らかい端の部分が空間の中に溶けこんでいくのを好んでいるようである。1981年の初個展以来、1994年東京で個展をするまで彼女は、床・天井・壁全て白く塗られ、自然光が入る京都の会場で作品発表をしてきた。それは西日が強烈に入る空間であり、時間によって会場となった空間の光は動いて行くために、作品が、ある時は強烈に影を作り、またある時はその部屋の空気と一体化したように見えなくなる瞬間があったりする。この会場での個展を重ねているうちに、彼女は、空間と物と観賞者との関係を考え出すようになってくる。それは作品を、ただギャラリーの空間においたり並べたりするのではなく、空間から感じとる空気感のようなものを、自分の漉いた紙を通して表現しようと試みるようになってくる。その瞬間から彼女は、京都を飛び出し日本の各地で空間との対話を始める。それは、1992年に開催された第15回ローザンヌタペストリービエンナーレ展（図版7）に入選した時期と重なる。この入選から彼女の作品は、海外でも紹介されるようになる。その中には、ただ単に日本の手漉きの和紙という素材を使っているからという、欧米からの物珍しさも加わっているような展覧会もあったようには思うが、（それはあくまで欧米から見られた視点であって）彼女は決してそのジャポニズムを売り込むような事は考えていない。あくまでも手で漉かれた紙の端の部分と、空間との関係をひたすら考えるために、作品発表を行っているのである。

自分で空間を探し、気に入った空間をまず調査し、そこから感じとる空気の流れ、光の流れを自分の作品とその

output has been produced from her own handmade paper. Using this material, a sense of ambiguity in the space in which the work is installed is heightened, owing to the frayed fibre edges of the paper, to its softness of texture, and to the formation of organic shapes which complement the artist's concept of installation. Let us now look at her sense for installation work more closely. Since 1981, when Ohgi had her first solo exhibition in Kyoto, she has shown a preference for a 'white cube' type of space, on condition that the rooms have sufficient daylight.

A space she has often exhibited in is *Gallery Gallery* in Kyoto, and in particular one of its rooms which faces west. The atmospheric light of the setting sun streaming in to this space creates an additional component, namely *time*. In a way, time as a subject has come to dominate Ohgi's installations, for instance the way in which, at a certain moment in a day, objects project a strong shadow on the wall, then later on the work appears to be absorbed into the space.

As she progressed with this way of working she began to associate her installation with the spectators. She became more interested in suggesting some dialogues between her work and the spectators through a space. Then Ohgi left Kyoto and began to make dialogues with spaces in other places in Japan. Her departure coincided with her work being nominated for exhibition at the 15th Lausanne International Tapestry Biennale [Cat. 7] in 1992, and with the gradual recognition of her work in the West.

Many exhibitions in which Ohgi has participated

3 | floating grass
at Gallery Gallery
1993

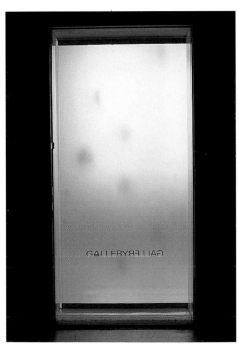

4 | fragmented light
at Gallery Gallery
| 1999

設置方法で表現しようとしている。それは依頼された空間からでも同じことを行っている。この空間や空気（環境）とかかわって行くという行為は、とても日本的ではないかと私は思っている。日本は、昔より空間や自然とともに暮らす生活をしていた。春は花を楽しみ、秋は月や虫の声を楽しみ、自分たちの生活の中に取り入れてきた。今となっては随分なくなってしまった、四季おりおりの日常でのイベントから得たものは、私たち日本の芸術家の奥深いところに残っているのではないかと思っている。そういう、自然との感覚的な交わりが出来るというものを持っている作家こそ、日本を離れたところでその特徴がいかせるのではないかと思っている。つまり欧米から見るとはるか遠いところに位置している、日本という国のアイデンティティを持っている作家こそが、世界に注目されるアーティストになりえると言うことではないだろうか。扇千花はこの要素をもっているからこそ、最近は欧米での展覧会に招待されるのだと私は思っている。それは、最初に書いた日本のあいまいさを表現している部分かもしれない。白とも黒ともはっきりしないもの。ぼんやりと空間の中で見え隠れする物。障子にうつされた影のような物。月の光を吸収した雪景色。夏の蛍などなど。これは元来、日本の人々が好むものでもある。それを彼女は、作品を発表することで彼女なりのセンスで表現している。

彼女の作品を見て、たよりない感覚を持つ人たちもいるかも知れない。これはまさに先に述べたような日本独特の感覚かも知れない。最近においては、漉いた紙を使わず、ギャラリーの内部に色セロファンを天井から吊るし、鑑賞者はギャラリーの中に入れず、ドアのガラス越しに作品を見るという空間構成をした作品 (図版4) を発表した。おまけにガラスには、半透明のシールが張ってあって、中はぼやけた感じにしか見ることが出来ない。鑑賞者は展覧会会場に差し込む日の光をたよりに、中になんとなく

introduced her work as being typically Japanese. However the idea of using Japanese paper as a way of presenting Japanese culture has hardly ever been a central thought of her work. Her concept is based rather on her personal interest in the ambiguity of the objects she creates expressed within a certain space.

Ohgi identifies spaces which complement her ideology. She develops a dialogue between herself and a space, endeavouring always to illuminate the flow of light and air. Her attitude of integrating herself in a space is in a way quintessentially Japanese. Traditionally, we in Japan have enjoyed a close relationship to nature, to the environment which surrounds us. For example, we derive enjoyment from the sight and fragrance of spring flowers, from the moonlight, from hearing the sounds of insects in the autumn. The environment forms a backdrop to our daily lives, and this poetic aspect of Ohgi's cultural identity is implicit in her works: something neither black nor white... floating in space... appearing through the sliding doors... snowy scenery bathed in moonlight... fireflies in summer.

Anyone not attuned to the sensitivities of Ohgi's Japanese environmental influence may miss some of the poetry and subtlety of her work. Recently the artist has been experimenting afresh. She has hung some coloured cellophane from the ceiling in a space, then she sealed the doorway using a sheet of translucent cellophane.[Cat. 4] In this way, the spectators only saw blurred images through the translucent screen, unless the cellophane was illuminated by the sunshine....

In England, there is a nation-wide event called 'Japan 2001 - Textural Space'. This is one of the events featuring contemporary Japanese textile art. This exhibition will tour for over a year throughout England. Two of Ohgi's work were selected and have been exhibited: this is the first time she has exhibited the same pieces in different spaces, rather than specifying a space for a piece. Although not a major transition in Ohgi's artistic development, this is nevertheless the beginning of an alternative way of working for the artist which will interest a wider audience.

Keiko Kawashima
Director:
Kyoto International Contemporary Textile Art Centre
(KICTAC);
Gallery Gallery

色のあるものが浮遊しながら動いている事に気がつく。そこには、ぼやけた空間のみが目に入ってくる。そしてしばらく観賞していると、鑑賞者は自然とその作品が醸し出す時間の流れの中に入りこんでいることに気がつく。これは、ある意味で彼女の目指しているあいまいな空間の到着点であったような気がしている。

2001年、英国では日本年と名うって、様々な展覧会が行われた。その1つの TEXTURAL SPACE 展という展覧会に彼女の作品が2点選ばれ、英国で展示されている。この展覧会は、1年をかけて英国の各地を巡回するものであるが、扇千花にとっては、特定の空間を意識せず（各会場で展示する空間は変わっていくから、特定の空間は意識出来ない）作品を展示することは、初めての挑戦だったと思う。これを機会に作品とその空間や環境に関する、彼女なりの意識が変化するかどうかは現段階ではさだかではないが、アーティストとして成長して行くことを私は期待している。

2001年8月19日、京都にて

京都インターナショナルコンテンポラリーテキスタイルアートセンター（KICTAC）主宰
ギャラリーギャラリー　主宰
川嶋　啓子

Keiko Kawashima (left) with Chika Ohgi (right)

Chika OHGI

5 | scene
1981

6 | thin ice
| 1994

I keep making, not knowing the consequence of my actions.

The answer for my questing will only be revealed when it is installed in a space.

なぜそうしようと思ったのかその意味もよくわからないまま、私は作業を続ける。

それを現実の空間に設置したとき、その理由が初めて私に明かされる。

7 | feather
1990

9 | dancing paper
| 1995

left:

8 | from hell to heaven
| detail
| 1992

overleaf:

10 | filled with light, water in the air
| 1995

I consider the space as important as my objects.

This is why I am interested in the edges of objects.

Each object has a very subtle boundary between the space and itself.

So the objects integrate themselves into the space.

私は物と空間を等価に設定したいと考えている。

そこで物と空間のあいだ、実在と不在の境界である物の輪郭に注目した。

私が作った物の輪郭はぼやけていて、空間との関係を曖昧にしている。

物と空間は物質的なグラデーションを繰り返し、どこからが物でどこまでが空間かわからなくなる。

そして私のインスタレーションは物と空間のあいだの曖昧な領域に満たされる。

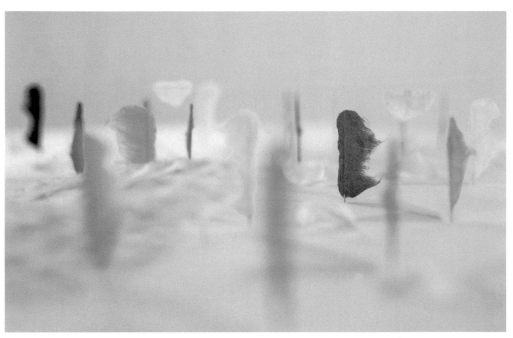

11 | fragment of paper
1997

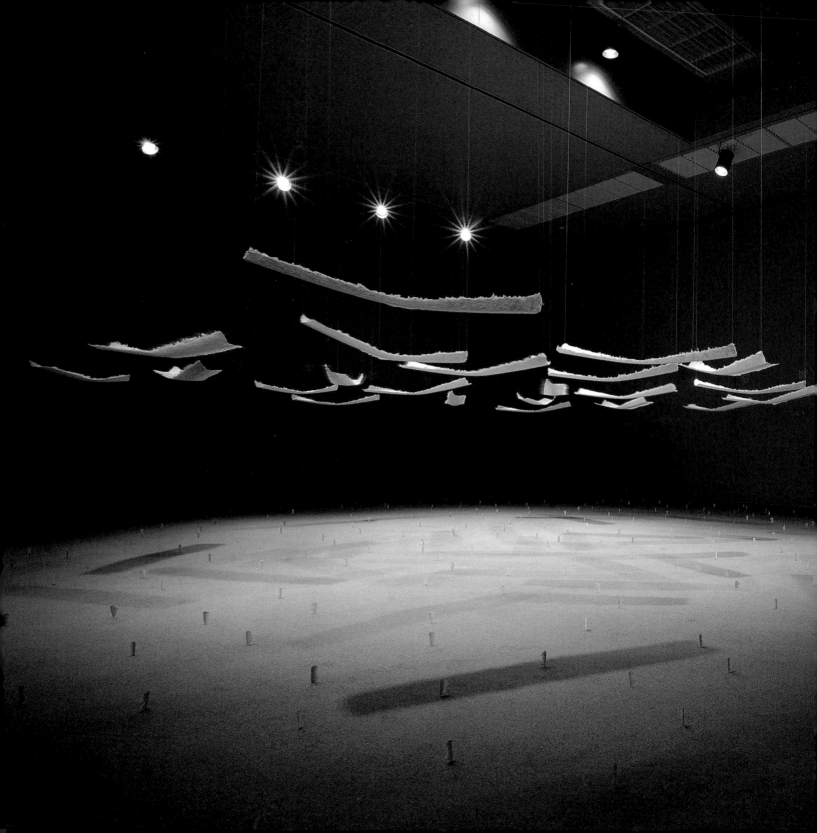

13 | filled with light, water in the air
1995

left:

12 | walking around the lake
1997

13 | filled with light,
water in the air
1995

15 | jellyfish garden
   | 1998

left:

14 | light on water, shadow under water
   | 2000

16 | from air to air
| 1991

My installations are gradually revealed to the spectators by the passage of time.

私のインスタレーションは観客が中で時間を過ごすことによって、ゆっくりと伝わっていった。

right:
13 | filled with light, water in the air
| 1995

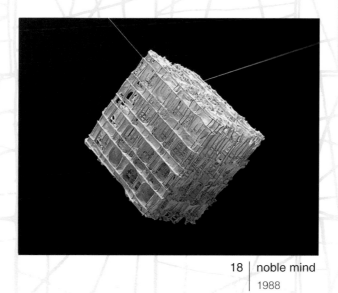

18 | noble mind
| 1988

left:
17 | water pillar
| 1995

20 | droplets of water
1996

21 | fragmented light
1997

22 | fragment of sound
1998

right:
23 | fragmented light
1997

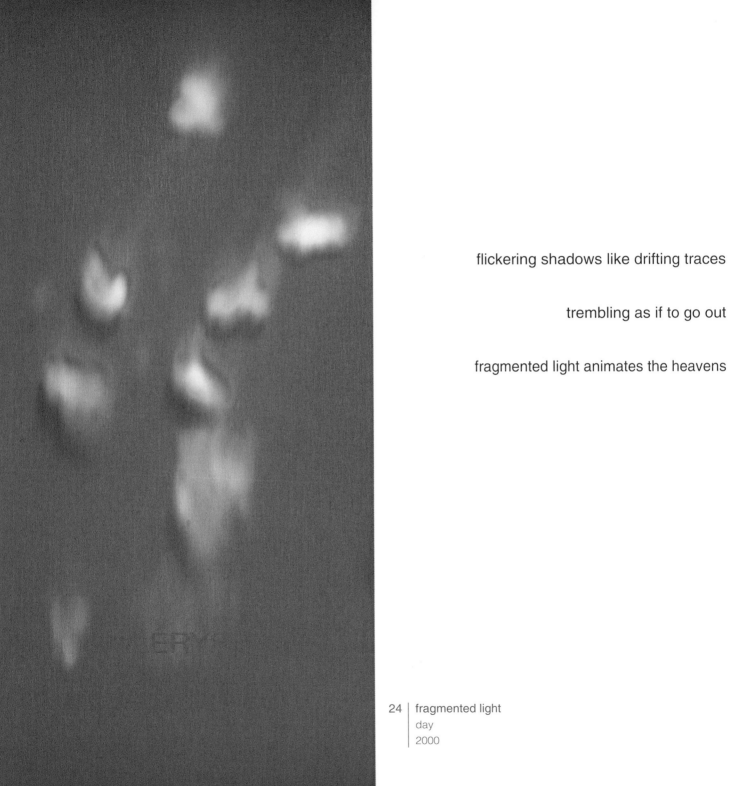

flickering shadows like drifting traces

trembling as if to go out

fragmented light animates the heavens

揺れる影の空間を漂う空気の感じ
そこにあるのに立ち消えてしまいそうな空気の感じ
光のかけらを宙に浮かべて

fragmented light
evening
2000

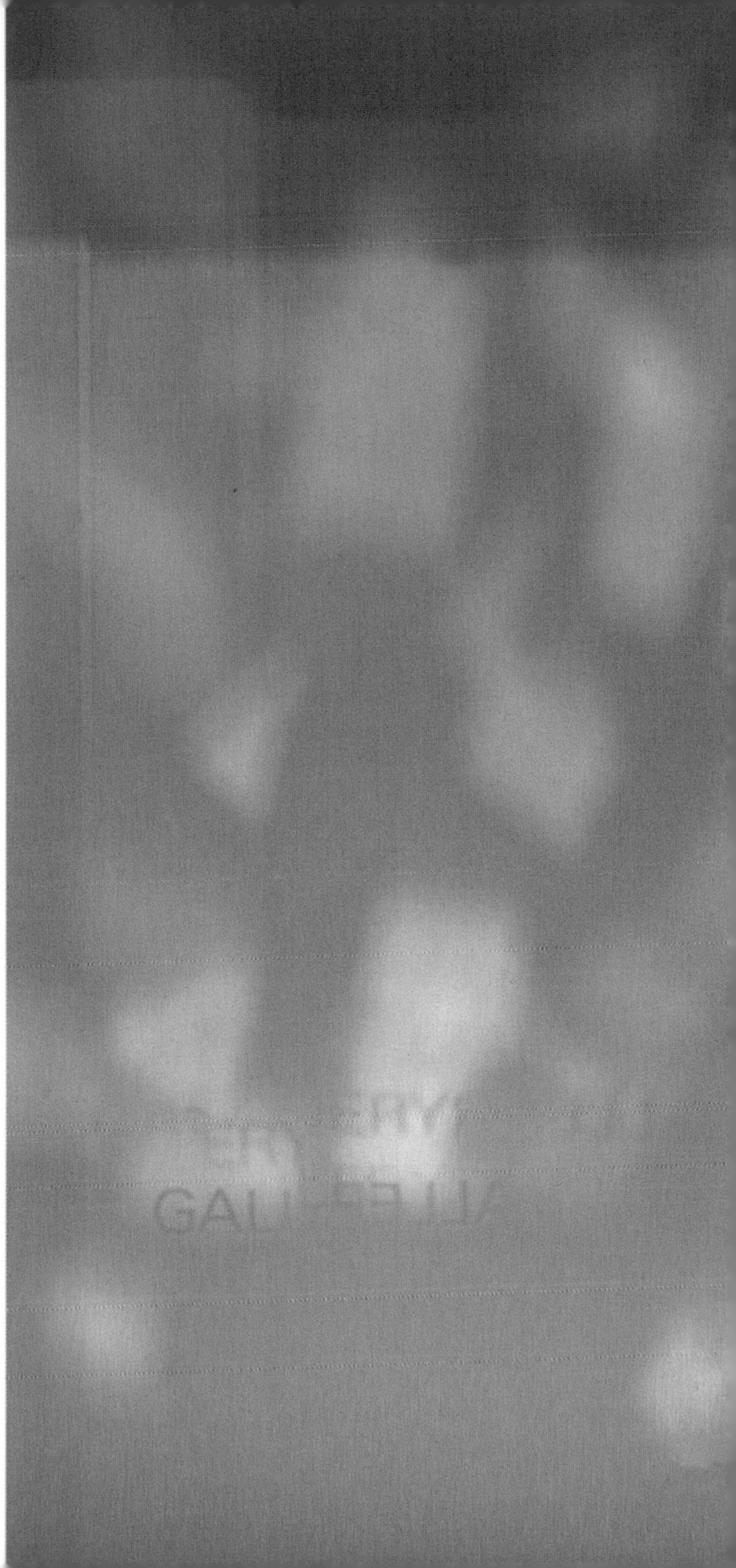

25 | where will the water and rainbow drift to?
| 2000

あるところとないところの間を見つめていた。
———— 扇 千花

Biography

Chika OHGI

1960　　Born in Osaka, Japan

1979-82 Postgraduate, Seian Women's College, Kyoto

1995-97 M.F.A. from Seika University, Kyoto

1998　　Artist-in-Residence, Canberra School of Art, ANU, Australia, supported by the Japan Foundation

1999　　Artist-in-Residence, Rias Ark Museum of Art, Miyagi

2000　　Research at Kyoto City University of Art

2001　　Artist-in-Residence, Sainsbury Centre, Norwich, England

Solo Exhibitions

1981　　Gallery Gallery, Kyoto, Japan (also in 1985-88, 90-93, 95, 96, 98-2000)

1985　　Gallery R II, Kyoto

1986　　Gallery CASA, Kyoto

1994　　Wacoal Ginza Art Space, Tokyo

　　　　Gallery Maronie, Kyoto (also in 1998)

1995　　Shoe Gallery Ota, Hyogo

1997　　Gallery Suzuki, Kyoto

　　　　X-port, Tokyo

1998　　Canberra Museum & Gallery, Australia

　　　　Exhibition Space Tokyo International Forum, Tokyo

1999　　Hirakata Municipal Gotenyama Art Center, Osaka

　　　　Exhibition Space Ecru + HM, Tokyo

　　　　Higashiyama Youth Center, Kyoto

2000　　za Gallery, Kyoto

　　　　Yamato Plaza, Tokyo

2001　　Gallery Ami and Gallery Kanoko, Osaka

　　　　ART SPACE LIFE blanc, Japan

Selected Group Exhibitions

1987   International Textile Competition '87 Kyoto, Kyoto International Conference Hall (also in 94, 97)

1988   7th International Biennial of Miniature Textile, Savaria Museum, Hungary

1989   9th Imadate Exhibition of Contemporary Paper Works, Imadate, Fukui (also in 90)

1992   15th International Lausanne Biennial, Musée Cantonal des Beaux-Arts, Lausanne, Switzerland

1993   4th Triennale International Mini Textile, Angers Museum, France

       International Prize, Hoppeland Art and Textile, Poperinge, Belgium

1994   light and shadow – Japanese Artists in Space, North Dakata Museum of Art

       Mini Art Textile, Como, Italy

1995   The 3rd In Our Hands International Competition, Nagoya Trade and Industry Center, Aichi

       The World of Paper, The National Museum of Art, Osaka

1996   Paper Art Fashion, Museum für Kunst und Gewerbe, Hamburg

       4th International Betonac Prize, Fiber Arts / Grand Prize, Cultural Centre de Bogaard, Belgium

1997   Shiga Annual '97 Paper Work, The Repro-Action of Form, The Museum of Modern Art Shiga

       Contemporary Art from Galleries '97, Osaka Contemporary Art Center, Osaka

1998   Art Exhibition of Selected Artists '98, Kyoto Municipal Museum

       IMAGINATIONS –Contemporary Japanese Textile Exhibition, Koen Art, Belgium

       Japanese Textile Miniature Exhibition folding, Canberra Museum and Gallery, Australia (tour)

1999   SOFA 1999 NYC, Seventh Regiment Armory, New York

2000   The Seaweed's paper & Four artists, Rias Ark Museum of Art, Miyagi

       Emerging Images, Mitaka Cty Arts Center, Tokyo

       folding, The Museum of Arts & Crafts, Itami, Hyogo

2001   Textile Art Postcard Exhibition, Gallery Gallery EX, Kyoto

       Textural Space – Contemporary Japanese Textile Art, Farnham, England (tour)

       Miniatures from Textural Space, Beardsmore Gallery, London

Paper Making Workshops

1997   Kyoto Seika University, Kyoto (also in 1998, 99)

1998   Primrose Park Art & Craft Centre, Sydney

Canberra School of Art, The Australian National University

Kawashima Textile School, Kyoto (also in 1999, 2000)

1999   Hirakata Municipal Gotenyama Art Center, Osaka

Wako University, Tokyo, Japan (also in 2000, 01)

Seian College of Art and Design, Kyoto (also in 2000)

2000   Higashiyama Youth Center, Kyoto

Mitaka Cty Arts Center, Tokyo

Rias Ark Museum of Art, Miyagi

za Gallery, Kyoto, Japan

Yokohama Museum of Art, Kanagawa

2001   Kyoto University of Art and Design, Kyoto

Sainsbury Centre for Visual Arts, Norwich

Itami Hall, Hyogo

Fukuoka Art Museum, Fukuoka

right:
photos by Chika Ohgi
in | Kyoto
Fukuoka
New York
Kesennuma
Beijing
Ayutthaya
Ho Chi Minh
London
Venice
Siena
Rome
1997-2001

List of works

No.	Title	Year	Technique	Materials
1	floating grass	1994	paper making	ganpi, bamboo
2	paper field	1986	burn	japanese paper, wood
3	floating grass	1993	paper making	kozo, cypress board
4	fragmented light	1999	own technique	translucent sheet, cellophane
5	scene	1981	own technique	japanese paper, blue water
6	thin ice	1994	paper making	ganpi, cotton thread
7	feather	1990	paper making, impressed leaf, natural dyeing	kozo, silver leaf, needle
8	from hell to heaven	1992	paper making, impressed leaf, dyeing	pulp, cotton thread, silver leaf
9	dancing paper	1995	paper making	kozo, cotton thread
10	filled with light, water in the air	1995	paper making	kozo, cotton thread
11	fragment of paper	1997	paper making	kozo, ganpi, pulp, cotton thread, needle
12	walking around the lake	1997	paper making	kozo, ganpi, cotton thread, cypress board, needle
13	filled with light, water in the air	1995	paper making	kozo, ganpi, cotton thread, ramie thread, cypress board
14	light on water, shadow under water	2000	paper making	algae paper, bamboo
15	jellyfish garden	1998	paper making	kozo, ganpi, silk thread, bamboo
16	from air to air	1991	paper making	pulp, jute thread, burned leaf
17	water pillar	1994	paper making	ganpi, ramie thread
18	noble mind	1988	paper making	pulp, cotton thread
19	fragmented light	1997	paper making	kozo, pulp, wire
20	droplets of water	1996	paper making	kozo, ramie thread
21	fragmented light	1997	ikat dyeing	feather, silk thread
22	fragment of sound	1998	own technique	charcoal, cotton thread
23	fragmented light	1997	paper making	kozo, ganpi, cotton thread, ramie thread, mirror
24	fragmented light	2000	own technique	sunlight (day), light (evening), water wind, mirror, cloth
25	where will the water and rainbow drift to?	2000	paper making, dyeing	kozo, cypress board

Dimensions	Exhibition, Gallery	Photographer	Page
80 x 80 x 15cm	North Dakata Museum of Art, USA	You. Kobayashi	5
90 x 135 x 10cm	International Textile Competition '87, Kyoto	Hiroshi Kimura	8
7 x 45 x 10cm x 21 pieces	Gallery Gallery, Kyoto	Koichi Nishimura	10
185 x 92cm	Gallery Gallery, Kyoto	You. Kobayashi	11
29 x 22 x 5cm x 72 pieces	Gallery Gallery, Kyoto		15
15 x 15 x 1cm	Wacoal Ginza Art Space, Tokyo	You. Kobayashi	16
10 x 6 x 0.2cm x 500 pieces	Gallery Gallery, Kyoto 15th International Lausanne Biennial	Akira Koike	17
3.5 x 40 x 0.2cm	Gallery Gallery, Kyoto	Koichi Nishimura	18
6 x 40 x 0.2cm x 60 pieces	Taka Shrine, Idecho, Kyoto	You. Kobayashi	19
6 x 40 x 0.2cm x 300 pieces	Ex-Meirin Elementary School, Kyoto	Koichi Nishimura	20
	postcard shot	You. Kobayashi	23
400 x 950 x 950cm	The Museum of Modern Art Shiga, Shiga	Yutaka Obata	24
380 x 1200 x 850cm	The National Museum of Art, Osaka	You. Kobayashi	25, 26, 31
1 x 150 x 150cm x 28 pieces	Rias Ark Museum of Art, Miyagi (public collection)	Tsutomu Koiwa	28
1 x 80 x 80cm x 50 pieces	Exhibition Space Tokyo International Forum	You. Kobayashi	29
30 x 30 x 1cm x 80 pieces	Gallery Gallery, Kyoto	Koichi Nishimura	30
300 x 61 x 61cm x 10 pieces	Gallery Maronie, Kyoto	You. Kobayashi	32
13 x 13 x 13cm	Gallery Gallery, Kyoto	Koichi Nishimura	33
234 x 450 x 330cm	The Museum of Kyoto	Koichi Nishimura (back)	34, 35
340 x 367 x 382cm	Gallery Gallery, Kyoto	You. Kobayashi	36
260 x 420 x 910cm	Gallery Suzuki, Kyoto	You. Kobayashi	36
300 x 686 x 257.5cm	Gallery Gallery, Kyoto	You. Kobayashi	36
133 x 910 x 130cm	The Museum of Kyoto	You. Kobayashi	37
195 x 92cm	Gallery Gallery, Kyoto	You. Kobayashi	38, 39
7 x 85 x 12cm	Mitaka Cty Arts Center, Tokyo	You. Kobayashi	40

height x width (x depth)

Other titles in this series

Vol 3: Caroline Broadhead (UK)
by Jeremy Theophilus
Shadows, windows, invisibility…
examine some of the inspirational
threads animating Britain's winner of
the Jerwood Prize for Textiles.
ISBN 1902015231

Vol 4: Chika Ohgi (Japan)
by Keiko Kawashima
Be enchanted by one of Kyoto's finest
artists working in installations with paper.
She composes her work using space itself
as an equal presence.
ISBN 1902015258

Vol 5: Anne Marie Power (Australia)
by Dr Juliette Peers
Textile artist, papermaker and sculptor,
Power plays upon the issues of cultural
trafficking and influences between
continent and continent.
ISBN 1902015266

Vol 6: Anne Wilson (USA)
by Tim Porges and Hattie Gordon
This important American artist uses human
hair, table linens and hand-stitching to probe
poignant personal memories and histories,
as well as evoking a subtle sense of landscape.
ISBN 1902015223

Vol 7: Alice Kettle (UK)
by Dr Jennifer Harris
Get up close and intimate with probably
the largest machine embroideries in the world
dating from 1997–2002, including a move
to landscape.
ISBN 1902015312

Vol 8: Helen Lancaster (Australia)
by Carolyn Skinner
The perilous fragility of nature, beautifully depicted
by an outstanding conceptual environmentalist using
embroidery and fabric manipulation.
ISBN 1902015290

Vol 9: Kay Lawrence (Australia)
by Dr Diana Wood Conroy
One of the world's top tapestry weavers, her recent
work negotiates issues about identity in textures
ranging from minimal to lush, from sensuous to spiky.
ISBN 1902015282

Vol 10: Joan Livingstone (USA)
by Gerry Craig
Livingstone's powerful installations incorporate felt,
stitch and epoxy resin. Professor of Fiber and Material
Studies at the School of the Art Institute, Chicago, she
is one of America's most important fiber sculptors.
ISBN 1902015274

Vol 11: Marian Smit (Netherlands)
by Marjolein v.d. Stoep
1st Prize winner in Third International Paper Triennal,
Switzerland, 1999. "Work of great simplicity
combining technique and poetry."
ISBN 1902015320

Vol 12: Chiyoko Tanaka (Japan)
by Lesley Millar
Tanaka's prized weavings are in public collections
around the world. A leading light from Kyoto,
her work is breathtaking and awe-inspiring.
ISBN 190201524X

still available:
Vol 1: Jilly Edwards (UK)
by Lene Bragger and Melanie Cook
ISBN 1902015207

Vol 2: Marian Bijlenga (Netherlands)
by Jack Lenor Larsen and Gert Staal
ISBN 1902015215

**visit www.arttextiles.com to order any of our titles
online or to view a list of our international stockists**